Lionel Messi

The Inspirational Story of Soccer (Football) Superstar Lionel Messi

Table of Contents

Introduction

Chapter 1: Youth & Family Life

Chapter 2: Professional Life

Chapter 3: Personal Adult Life

Chapter 4: Philanthropic/Charitable Acts

Chapter 5: Legacy, Potential & Inspiration

Conclusion

Introduction

As the title implies, this is a short book about [The Inspirational Story of Football Superstar Lionel Messi] and how he rose from his life in Argentina to become one of today's leading and most-respected football players. In his rise to superstardom, Lionel, also affectionately called "Leo", has inspired not only the youth, but fans of all ages throughout the world.

This book also portrays the struggles Lionel has had to overcome during his early childhood years and his teen years to become what he is today. A notable source of inspiration is Leo's service to the community and his strong connection with the fans of the sport. He continues to serve as a humble, mild-mannered, transcendent superstar in a sport that needs it.

Combining incredible mental fortitude, impeccable mechanics, an aggressive play style, and high football IQ, Leo has shown the ability to dominate a match. From being a young boy with a hormonal deficiency to becoming one of the greatest football players of all time, you'll learn how this man has risen in the ranks.

Thanks again for grabbing this book. Hopefully, you can take some lessons from Lionel "Leo" Messi's story and apply them to your own life.

Chapter 1:

Youth & Family Life

Luis Lionel Andres Messi, popularly known today as Leo Messi, was welcomed into the world on June 24th, 1987 in the city of Rosario in the province of Santa Fe in Argentina. He was born to father, Jorge Horacio Messi, and mother, Celia Maria Cuccittini. His father worked in a steel factory and ran the local football club Grandoli, where Leo officially started his childhood years as a football player, while Leo's mother worked as a part-time cleaner. Although Leo was born in Argentina and became a citizen of Spain later in his life, his paternal and maternal ancestors are from Italy and Spain, respectively.

Leo also has three siblings, two older brothers and a sister - Rodrigo, Matias, and Maria Sol. As a child, Leo was the mischievous one amongst the siblings, but only when he was at home with his family. Outside the Messi residence, everyone knew him differently. When the family was home, nobody wanted to play cards with the young Leo, because he would mix up all the cards on the table whenever he lost. This was received by his father as an early sign that Leo has an intense desire to win.

Because Leo was also the youngest boy of the family, he tried to keep up with his older brothers from the time he learned to walk. Inevitably, he soon followed along whenever his brothers would play football with their friends. Even though he was the youngest and the smallest on the field, Leo instinctively knew how to compete harder to compensate for his physical disadvantages - something that would stay with him throughout his life.

At Leo's primary school, Colegio Heneral Las Heras, he was known by his classmates and his teachers to be shy and reserved, especially in the classroom. However, it was inevitable for him to show his natural football skills whenever he played with his classmates on the school grounds. Anyone who picked him as a teammate would also choose him as the team leader. He even received the moniker "The Flea" from his schoolmates. This name was given to Leo as an acknowledgement of his incredible football handling skills, despite his small frame. As "The Flea", Leo was picked as a member of a school football team over some boys who were older than him.

During his stay at Colegio Las Heras, the entire school knew Leo trained, played, and won for several local football clubs, but Leo was never seen showing off or heard bragging about his achievements to anyone. Whenever Leo's proud mother visited the school, bringing with her Leo's football medals and trophies, he would quickly stop her where she was standing and ask her not to show and let everyone know his winnings.

When Leo was about to turn five years old, he met his first football coach, Salvador Aparicio. On their first meeting, Leo went with his parents and his maternal grandmother, Celia Oliveira, to watch his brother Rodrigo play for a local club. Leo was noticed by Salvador playing across the pitch alone and became curious of the boy dribbling with the ball impressively. Coincidentally, Salvador's team was lacking one member that evening.

The coach then approached Leo's mother and asked if her son could fill in for the no-show that evening. She was hesitant, but after Salvador convinced her that Leo would not be forced to do anything special while in the pitch, she finally agreed. But without the influence of Leo's grandmother to her daughter that evening, Leo would have missed being discovered at an early age.

While Leo considers his brothers to be instrumental in developing his skill in football, he acknowledges with pride his greatest influence – his grandmother. Every time Leo scores a goal, even until this day, he would point his fingers to the sky as a tribute to her.

During Leo's stint on the pitch that evening, he did not score a goal, but Salvador was quick to notice what else happened, which marked the beginning of his journey as one of the world's most successful football players. On the pitch, the first time the ball came across Leo's way, he just let it pass. But the second time it hit his left leg, he ran across the pitch, dribbled, and allowed no one to get in his way. From that point on, Salvador made Leo a regular player for his youth team.

Whenever Leo attended practice with his teammates at the football training center, Newell's Old Boys club, he would be seen practicing alone. No one wanted to play with him, because he was too good for his teammates, who were the same age as him. So Carlos Marconi, another one of Leo's first football coaches and now the academy director of Newell's Old Boys, fielded him with bigger boys. Like the size of his teammates did not matter, Leo simply dribbled the ball past the bigger players on the field and scored goals, as if he was playing alone. Carlos thought of adding Leo to a team already playing competitively. With Carlos' and his new teammates' confidence in him, Leo would score at least five goals every time he was on the pitch.

One popular story from Carlos about Leo was the young boy's exceptional self-motivational skills. Leo, despite always being tired with his football practice and matches, remained very picky with food. But Carlos knew his favorite - chocolate biscuits. Carlos motivated Leo to play well, even in practice, by rewarding Leo with a piece of biscuit every time he scored a goal.

But the reward was too easy for Leo to get. So Carlos leveled up the challenge and told Leo that if he scored a goal with his head, he would be rewarded with two pieces of chocolate biscuits, instead of just one. Carlos thought Leo would have difficulties as he was small, even for his age. However, Leo could deliver. In one of their drills, Leo dribbled past his teammates with the ball as he always did, and upon reaching the goal, he quickly flicked it with his foot and hit it towards the goal with his head.

Leo was six years old when he officially joined the Newell's Old Boys. While with the club, the team only lost one match in four years. This feat gave them the name "The Machine of '87", as they were all born during that year.

In most of their matches, Leo's teammates tried to take the load off of him and provided him with options to win the match. But Leo planned and scored most of the team's goals. In his six years of playing for the club, Leo scored close to 500 goals.

In interviews, after they had long been with different careers, "The Machine of '87" only have good words for Leo. Until this day, they give most of the credit for their team's success to Leo, looked up to him as their leader, and even called him "The Architect."

It was also during Leo's stint with the Newell's Old Boys when highly-acclaimed clubs in Europe and South America noticed him. However, something else also became noticeable in him. While he and his teammates showed dominance on the field and continuously developed their football skills, Leo remained small for his age.

His doctors eventually diagnosed Leo with a growth hormone deficiency when he was eleven years old and prescribed him a treatment. This treatment lasted for a few years, until the family could no longer afford the expenses. The health insurance Leo's father had could only cover a maximum of two years for his treatment, which was almost $1,000 USD a month. Initially, Newell's Old Boys covered part of the cost, but discontinued the support later on due to restraints.

Still lucky, Leo was then scouted by RiverPlate, a club based in Buenos Aires. For some time, he had the means to pay for his treatment, but the support also had to be stopped by Riverplate because of Argentina's economic collapse.

Leo must have been lucky that he had been noticed by FC Barcelona when they sought support from their relatives in Catalona, Spain. There had been hesitation from the academy's board of directors to sign Leo, because he was very young and a foreigner. But a later directive from the academy eventually had him sign with them. FC Barcelona's sporting director, Carles Rexach, was so excited and overly impressed with Leo's physical skills and mental approach towards the sport that he wrote the young man's contract on a napkin to make sure he got on board immediately.

Part of the agreement allowed Leo to join and train at the FC Barcelona Youth Academy's La Masia, while they paid for Leo's hormonal treatment. At thirteen, Leo saw himself moving with his family across the Atlantic Ocean to Spain and lived in a small apartment near Camp Nou, the academy's football stadium.

During Leo's first year with La Masia, he was rarely in the pitch because of conflicts with his transfer from Newell's Old Boys to the academy. He was only fielded in Catalan leagues and friendly matches. Also, he hardly interacted with his teammates. Because he was reserved by nature and was homesick due to his mother and siblings moving back to Rosario the same year, affected his interaction with his teammates to where some thought he was literally mute.

Despite dealing with the culture shock of being on a new continent, Leo could still hone his football skills. In 2002, he enrolled with the Spanish Football Federation and played in competitions. This is also when he developed close friendships with his teammates, among them were Gerard Pique and Cesc Fabregas.

2002 was a great year for Leo's health and career in Spain. His hormonal treatment had been completed, and he became an essential part of what was dubbed as Barcelona's "Baby Dream Team", a group of promising football players in the same age bracket as Leo.

From 2000 to 2003, Leo saw himself playing with different FC Barcelona junior teams –

Infantile B, Cadetes B, and Cadetes A. In his first full season (2002-2003) with Cadetes A, he made a record- 36 goals in 30 matches. This made him the top scorer for the season. Also, his feat contributed to Cadetes A winning an unprecedented treble (three trophies in a single season) in the league and winning in the Catalan and Spanish clubs.

In a match during the season, Leo suffered from a cheekbone injury. Because his team could not afford to lose the finals against Espana in the Copa Catalunya Cup the following week, he would be fielded at the start, but with a plastic mask on his face to protect himself from further injury.

On the pitch, the mask hindered Leo from playing, so he took the protection off his face and scored 2 goals in 10 minutes (also referred to as a brace in football) before he was substituted. His team won with a score of 4-1. This act of Leo is well-known to many football fans as the "Partido de la Mascara" or the "Final of the Mask."

At the end of the season, Leo saw his friends, Pique and Fabregas, leaving for England, while he stayed with Barcelona and declined an offer from Arsenal, an English football club based in Holloway, London.

After almost being released in 2003 because of financial restrictions from Barcelona, Leo proved the club's decision to keep him was right, when he played well in the 2003-2004 season. His hard work set him a record of playing for five teams during the season. Apart from this record, four pre-season international tournaments named him player of the tournament.

In that season, Leo's fourth full season with Barcelona, he debuted in the first team via a friendly match against Porto, held on November 16th, 2003. During the match, Leo joined the team on the pitch at the 75th minute and highly impressed the technical staff with his performance – two chances and one shot at the goal.

After the match, Leo trained for the first team weekly and for the Barcelona B reserve team daily. In the training, he became friends with Ronaldinho, who was an FC Barcelona star. The friendship with Ronaldinho helped Leo to transition smoothly to the first team. Since he was extensively training for the first team and the reserve teams, he only got to play in one match with Juvenil B, another youth division team of FC Barcelona. But because of his consistently strong performance, despite being absent in the youth division for some time, he was still promoted to Juvenil A, where he scored twenty-one goals in fourteen matches.

Leo gained more field experience when he joined Barcelona C, FC Barcelona's third team. He saved this team from being relegated in the Tercera Division, when he contributed five goals in the ten matches he played. These goals included a hat-trick (scoring three goals in a match) he achieved in just eight minutes during a Spanish Cup match. Leo pulled off the rare hat-trick, despite Sevilla's Sergio Ramos, who man-marked him throughout the match.

Leo became more unstoppable and soon joined Barcelona B with his buy-out clause increased to €80 million. However, he failed to score while with the team in the Segunda Division B, despite having played in five matches. He was deemed weaker compared to his teammates in Barcelona B. The latter were not only taller, but also more experienced than he was. Leo knew of this and pushed himself to put on more muscle mass and improve his overall strength. Before the end of the season, he returned and played for Juvenil B, helping the youth team win the league.

With Barcelona B, Leo played in seventeen matches and scored goals in six. Although he had not played for the first team since his debut in the match against Porto, he became a member of the first team with the help of the team's senior players, led by Ronaldinho.

On October 16th, 2004, Leo was finally chosen by Frank Rijkaard to play against RCD Espanyol. Frank positioned him in the right wing against his wishes and saw Ronaldinho play in the left wing instead. However, this did not hinder Leo from delivering his game. He could still cut through the center of the field, kick with his dominant left foot, and shoot the ball in the goal.

It was the 82nd minute of the match against RCD Espanyol, when Leo was called to join his teammates on the pitch. This appointment made Leo the third-youngest player to play for Barcelona, and the youngest club member to play in La Liga. He was only seventeen years and a few months old.

A month before he turned eighteen years old, Leo scored his first senior goal for Barcelona in a game against Albacete Balompie via assist from Ronaldinho. This made him the youngest player to score for the club in a La Liga match. For the record, Leo only played 77 minutes for the first team in the 2004-2005 season as a substitute in 9 matches.

Also, the team was only in their second season under Rijkaard when they won the league for the first time after six years. It was also during the season that Leo debuted in the UEFA Champions League via an appointment from Rijkaard. The debut was in a match against Shakhtar Donetsk, a Ukrainian football club.

While Leo's early success was a testament of his hard work, Rijkaard's confidence in the young man cannot be understated. Leo has since said, regarding Rijkaard, he will "never forget the fact that he launched my career".

The young Leo always aspired to play for La Albiceleste, Argentina's national football team. Sparked further with his feeling of homesickness, he accepted the offer to play for the Argentine youth team in 2004 and to represent his country of birth in the FIFA World Championships later. This was despite Carles Rexach and the Spanish Football Federation already pursuing him as early as 2003.

Leo is both a Spanish and an Argentine citizen, so both countries wanted his representation in the international football arena. However, the Argentine Football Association was quick to organize under-20 friendly matches with Uruguay and Panama to seal an agreement with Leo, before Spain could make theirs. It was in the match against Paraguay that Leo debuted as a player of the Argentine team. He scored a goal and provided two assists in the match, which led to their win with a score of 8-0.

After this match, Leo also represented Argentina in the FIFA World Cup Youth Championships qualifier, held in Colombia in 2005. Although he was only fielded as a substitute in six of the nine matches, he redeemed himself with the match against Venezuela and Brazil. He scored a goal in the game against Brazil, helping his team win with a score of 2-1. This win placed them third in the South American Youth Championships, and secured them a position in the youth division of the World Cup.

During the 2005 World Cup Youth Championships held in the Netherlands, Leo was never a part of the Argentine team's starting lineup for its match against the United States. The team lost by a score of 1-0. The team's senior players felt the absence of Leo cost them the match. After convincing the team manager, Francisco Ferraro, the team saw Leo play in the group stage and helped them win against Egypt and Germany.

During the knockout stage, Leo tied the match (referred to as an equaliser in football) against Colombia and contributed a goal to their win against the favorite, Spain. In their winning match against Brazil, which led them to the finals, he provided the team its first goal.

Before the finals, Leo was acknowledged as the tournament's best player and received his first Golden Ball. To further Argentina's winning streak, he scored two goals via penalty kicks and led the team to win the World Cup Youth Championships trophy against Nigeria. Leo ended his first international tournament as the top scorer with six goals.

His achievements in the 2005 World Cup Youth Championships had Argentines celebrating their fifth championship and had them believing that Leo was the next Diego Maradona.

Chapter 2:

Professional Life

While Leo Messi's outstanding achievements in junior football were highly-recognized, his actual debut in the senior division did not kick off well.

On August 17th, 2005, the senior manager and head coach of the Argentine team, Jose Peckerman, invited him to play in a friendly match against the Hungarian national team. He was appointed to the pitch at the 65th minute of the game, but was sent off at the 67th minute mark. One of the Hungarian players grabbed his shirt, and while he tried to shake the player off him, Leo accidentally struck the player instead. The referee called it a foul against him and cited that he elbowed the opposing player intentionally. There were reports that Leo did not take the referee's decision lightly and was found crying in the dressing room.

A month later, Leo still returned to the Argentine national football team and even declared it as his second debut. Although the team lost in the World Cup qualifiers against Paraguay, Leo redeemed himself and the team via the qualifying match against Peru. He secured the win by contributing a goal at the penalty shootout.

On Leo's eighteenth birthday, it was announced that Barcelona had decided to update Leo's contract and pay him as a first team member going forward. The contract made him a first team player until 2010. Although this was twenty-four months short, compared to his prior contract, his buyout clause was increased to €150 million.

Fans were also excited for Leo's future, even giving him a standing ovation during his first substitution in front of the Camp Nou home crowd. This happened on August 24th, 2005, during the team's pre-season competition, the Joan Gamper Trophy, in a match against Juventus. With his first Champions League match, Leo showed strong chemistry with the legendary Ronaldinho.

In less than three months, Leo again signed an updated contract with Barcelona. Instead of 2010, Leo's contract expiry had been extended until 2014. This was the response of Barcelona towards bids to buy Leo out from the club. The most publicized bidder was Inter-Milan Club, willing to buy Leo from Barcelona with his wages at the time tripled.

Because of legal issues with his citizenship and his status with the Spanish Football Federation, Leo did not play for La Liga until he obtained his Spanish citizenship on September 26th, 2005, a showing of his commitment to Barcelona.

After securing the legality of his career in Spain, Leo, with Ronaldinho and Samuel Eto'o, came to be known as the attacking trio on the football field. Leo slowly made himself the first choice on the right wing, Ronaldinho on the left, and Samuel as the striker.

One of the most memorable highlights of Leo's first La Liga was his first El Clasico match. In Spanish football, a match between strongest rivals, FC Barcelona and Real Madrid, is referred to as El Clasico. Another highlight was his performance in their match against Chelsea, during the Champions League Round of 16. Leo's performance in this round is said to be his best match in the league during the season.

Leo scored eight more goals during his twenty-five appearances and one Champions League goal in six matches. However, this season did not end on his terms, as he suffered a muscle tear in his right thigh during a second round Champions League match against Chelsea. On a positive note, the team finished the season as the champions of both Spain and Europe.

Leo wanted to join Barcelona in the finals of the Champions League, so he worked hard to regain his fitness. Unfortunately, on the day of the finals, he was found still unfit and could not play. Barcelona won the Champions League held in Paris, but Leo was disappointed and chose not to celebrate the victory with the team.

Leo's regular appearances were also part of his preparations for the World Cup, which officially began for his team when they won against Croatia in a friendly match. He scored a goal in this game.

Despite not being fully recovered from his thigh injury, Leo partook in the 2006 World Cup for Argentina. He was lucky to have been chosen for the squad, but watched Argentina's opening match against Ivory Coast from the bench.

After the team's victory in the first match, Leo finally found himself fielded in the second match against Serbia and Montenegro. At the time of his appointment at the 75th minute, he became the youngest Argentine to represent the country in the World Cup. After only a few minutes after his appointment, he assisted Hernan Crespo on a goal, and then scored one for himself. This goal made Leo the youngest player to score a goal in this World Cup held in Germany and the third-youngest to score a goal in the history of the tournament.

During the knockout stage, when some of the starter players were asked to rest, Leo again played with the team against the Netherlands, which ended in a 0-0 draw. The team still won the match, based on goal difference (total goals scored in the tournament minus goals conceded).

The win against the Netherlands allowed the team to advance to the Round of 16. In their match against Mexico, Leo was fielded at the 84th minute, when the game was tied at 1-1. Argentina needed to score another goal within the extra time to proceed to the next round. While Leo appeared to have scored a goal within the extra time, it was ruled out as an offside. The team advanced to the quarterfinals and played against Germany.

In the quarterfinal match against Germany, Peckerman decided not to put Leo in the pitch, and Argentina eventually lost to Germany in a penalty shootout, in a score of 4-2. This ended the team's run in the World Cup. Back in Argentina, Peckerman's decision not to let Leo play was largely criticized. Argentines believed that if Leo was only fielded in the match, the team would have advanced further.

The 2006-2007 season marked Leo's first as a regular first team player for Barcelona. With his playing time, he saw his improvements in all of the major statistical categories, despite the obvious decline in FC Barcelona's overall performance. Across all competitions during the campaign, he shot 17 goals in 36 matches. However, the injury bug bit again in mid-

November, when Leo broke his metatarsal in a game against Real Zaragoza. He was forced to take three months away from competition to fully heal.

When Leo recovered from his injury, he went back to playing with his team during the Champions League final 16 rounds match against Liverpool. Unfortunately, they suffered a loss and failed to hold on to the championship trophy for 2006.

One of the highlights of Leo's season was his first hat-trick in an El Clasico on March 10th, 2007. It was the first time in 12 years someone posted a hat trick in an El Clasico. However, the match with Real Madrid proved to be one of the most challenging, as they were equalized thrice, ending the game in a 3-3 draw.

Despite missing so much time due to injury, Leo finished the season on a hot streak. He scored eleven goals in the final fourteen matches of the season, and his season total was fourteen goals in twenty-six matches. Another highlight of Leo's career during the 2006-2007 season happened on April 18th, 2007, when he also scored a brace in the Copa del Rey semifinal match against Getafe CF.

From the right side, near the halfway mark, Leo ran a distance of 200 feet with the ball past five defenders, kicked the ball from an angle, and scored. This was a move similar to Maradona's "Goal of the Century." Deco, Leo's teammate, even called it the best goal he had ever seen in his life.

In another match against Espanyol, Leo once again proved himself the rightful successor of Maradona by replicating his goal move, popularly known as the "Hand of God." Leo launched himself on the ball and led it past the opponent's goalkeeper with his hand as Maradona's hand was positioned, when he did it many years ago.

However, these unbelievable goals did not improve the overall performance of Leo's team. Apart from Leo having been rested during a match against Getafe in the second leg of the Copa del Rey Cup, Barcelona also lost the Champion's League from Real Madrid due to lower goal average. The season ended with Rijkaard moving Leo to the right wing, giving him more room to cut into the center of the pitch, and provided more opportunities for his left foot.

As he was slowly rising in global popularity, Leo received even more praise during the 2007 Copa America. During a 4-1 victory over the United States, he played beautifully as a playmaker, setting up teammates and creating shots for himself. Argentina then won the second game against Colombia, in which Leo was an offensive force, once again.

During the knockout stage match against Paraguay in the American Cup, Leo entered the field in the last 25 minutes. Fortunately, Leo could assist the team in shooting their only goal to win in the group and move on to the quarterfinals.

In the quarterfinal round against Peru, Leo scored one goal out of the four that allowed Argentina to advance to the semifinals. The team was once again on a winning streak. In the semifinal match against Mexico, Leo contributed a goal to bring the team's total goals to three against Mexico's zero. This paved their way to the championship round.

Argentina literally ended the final match against the heavily favored Brazil empty-handed, with a score of 0-3. Argentine fans were, once again, disappointed with their home team, but not with Leo. Argentines cited Leo as being the youngest in the bunch. Leo was named "Young Player of the Tournament", boosting his fan following even further.

2007 served as Leo's breakout year of sorts, as he was nominated for a FIFA FIFPro World XI Player Award and received personal endorsements from many of the great current and former players around the world. He finished third in the 2007 Ballon d'Or, after Cristiano Ronaldo, and Kaka, and second in the FIFA World Player of the Year, behind Kaka.

After he reached his 100th official match with Barcelona, Leo suffered another muscle tear in his left thigh during a Champions League match against Celtic FC. After he had fully recuperated from the injury, he returned and scored two goals for Barcelona to win the match against Celtic FC. This happened during the last 16 rounds of the league.

Leo still became the top scorer of the league with six goals under his record. Unfortunately, Leo had another injury during the return leg of the league on March 4th, 2008. Despite the injury and the warning from the medical staff, Rijkaard still appointed him at the pitch, which was not received well by his teammate, Carlos Puyol. Carlos directed his criticism towards the media, accusing them of pressuring the young Leo to play in every match - rather than taking his long term health into consideration.

The injuries and the criticism from a teammate seemed to have done no good for the team. At the end of the Champions League season, Barcelona was empty-handed. Barcelona received a semifinal upset from the champions of that year, Manchester United, only to place third in the league. But still, Leo's totals were an impressive sixteen goals and thirteen assists throughout all competitions.

The year 2008 also saw Leo conquer the sport during the Summer Olympics in Beijing. Leo did not take the easy route to the Olympics though. He was barred legally from representing Argentina at the Olympics by FC Barcelona, because the international sports event coincided with the schedule of the qualifying matches for the Champions League season 2008 and 2009. Soon enough though, the newly-appointed coach of Barcelona, Pep Guardiola, interfered with the club's decision and allowed Leo to join the Argentine national football team headed by its coach, Sergio Batista.

Argentina easily led the group by winning their opening match with the Ivory Coast, 2-1. Leo scored one of the two goals and assisted on the other. In the qualifying match for the quarterfinals against Australia, Leo and his team won again with one goal against the opponent's zero. While Leo took a rest during the match against Serbia, the team still won, putting them at the top of their group.

Argentina battled it out in the field with the Netherlands in the quarterfinals. Leo contributed a goal and assisted with the second strike during the extra time, allowing them to advance in the finals, two goals against the Netherlands' lone goal.

In the semifinal round, Argentina, once again, faced their popular rival, Brazil, but won the match this time, by a score of three to zero. In the finals, the team defeated Nigeria with a goal assisted by Leo. The goal and the win gave Leo his first Olympic gold medal. This absolute dominance on the global stage was a big moment in terms of Leo's popularity, as the world saw a star emerge right before its eyes.

After Ronaldinho's emotional departure from Barcelona, Leo inherited the number ten jersey. He finished second in the 2008 FIFA World Player of the Year award and third in the IFFHS World's Best Playmaker Award for the second straight year.

With external pressure building from the media, Leo answered the challenge to take his game to the next level in the 2008-2009 season. He scored a hat-trick against Atletico Madrid at the Copa del Rey and then a brace to defeat Racing Santander in a come-from-behind effort. In early April, he put up another brace against Bayern Munich during a Champions League game, setting a mark of eight goals in the competition. Then, he raised his season's goal total to thirty-six, after scoring another brace against Real Madrid.

Team success soon followed, as Barcelona won the Copa del Rey in mid-May. In Leo's first Copa del Rey match, he scored and assisted twice in the 4-1 victory. The team won La Liga and the Champions League. In doing so, Barcelona had become the first Spanish club to win the treble.

With nine goals scored, Leo became the youngest top scorer in the history of the Champions League. His personal accolades include winning the UEFA Club Forward of the Year and Footballer of the Year awards. Perhaps most importantly, the team showed incredible chemistry with its trio of Leo, Samuel Eto'o, and Ronaldinho's replacement, Thierry Henry, with a combined score of one hundred goals between them.

Coming from such an incredible season, Barcelona management came to an agreement with Leo as soon as possible. In mid-September, Leo and the club agreed to a new contract that would last until 2016, including a buy-out clause. Besides this new contract, Leo finally broke through in the Ballon d'Or race, coming in first place, ahead of Ronaldo. He finished in second place in the IFFHS World's Best Playmaker Award, behind his teammate, Xavi.

With so much happiness and praise around him, it would be only human nature for Leo to rest on his laurels. However, what makes him one of the all time greats is that he is never satisfied with his play, always looking for ways to improve and take his game to the next level. Leo's work ethic, still alive and well from his childhood, continued to drive him day in and day out.

As the 2009-2010 season began, Leo was moved from right winger to the center of the front line. It seemed risky for Barcelona to tweak what was already working, but Leo soon thrived in this new role. By mid-December, Barcelona had won the 2009 World Cup, thanks to Leo's winning goal in the final game. He was given the FIFA World Player of the Year award just two days later, marking the first time an Argentine had received the honor.

January saw Leo post a hat-trick in a 5-0 rout of CD Tenerife and get his 100th club goal in a match against Sevilla FC. Soon after, he scored another hat trick in a 3-0 victory over Valencia CF and once more, versus Real Zaragoza. This run made Leo the first player in Barcelona history to post consecutive hat-trick games in La Liga play.

Just when he was getting used to dropping a "three piece" fairly often, Leo bested himself by scoring all four goals in a 4-1 victory over Arsenal in the Champions League quarterfinals. By doing so, he overtook Rivaldo as the club's all-time leading goal scorer in the competition. His legend continued to grow, when he scored a brace in the final match of the season, tying Ronaldo's club record of thirty-four goals. In a landslide, he was announced as La Liga's Player of the Year for the second consecutive time. In all competitions, during the 2009-2010 season, Leo scored forty-seven goals and assisted eleven times, tying Ronaldo's goal mark.

While wearing the number ten for Argentina, Leo scored four goals during the South American 2010 World Cup qualifying process. In Argentina's World Cup matches, he was a part of each of the goals in a 4-1 victory over Korea Republic. Then, he captained Argentina in a victory over Greece, in which he was part of both of the team's goals. Argentina's World Cup run came to a screeching halt against Germany, as they lost 0-4 in the quarterfinal round.

Leo started his 2010-2011 season with a hat-trick in the first game against Sevilla FC. In mid-September, Leo experienced an ankle injury as the result of a tackle during the 92nd minute of a match. Because of the awkward collision, it was initially feared that Leo had broken his ankle. However, after an MRI, it was shown he had only suffered sprains in the ligaments of his right ankle. Upon returning, Leo scored another hat-trick in an 8-0 blowout of UD Algeria. The second of Leo's three goals put his La Liga career total at one hundred.

Leo was awarded the Ballon d'Or, once again, and was also nominated for a great deal of other awards. Most importantly for him, his personal dominance was also translating into team success. In February, Barcelona set a record for the most consecutive league wins, with sixteen. After going through a month-long slump in which he scored no goals at all, Leo posted a brace against UD Almeria. Despite his long run without a goal, Leo's second goal against Almeria tied his previous season's total of forty-seven for the season.

He then surpassed his previous year's record after scoring the winning goal in a Champions League game against Shakhtar Donetsk, making him the highest scorer in a single season in club history. Leo's La Liga campaign ended with thirty-one goals scored, and he was runner-up to

Ronaldo for the Pichichi trophy. He also finished the league season with eighteen assists, tops in the league.

Upon reaching the championship game of the 2011 Copa del Rey, Barcelona was defeated by Real Madrid in the final match. Leo and Ronaldo were joint-top scorers in the tournament, scoring seven apiece. After a disappointing end to Copa del Rey, Leo showed brilliance in the Champions League, scoring a brace in a 2-0 victory, avenging Real Madrid and the match-clinching goal of the Champions League final. The victory gave Barcelona its third title in six years. By the end of the season, Leo had scored fifty-three goals and assisted on twenty-four in all competitions combined.

Leo's hot streak against Real Madrid continued into the 2011-2012 season, as he started the season by helping Barcelona defeat Madrid, 5-4, on aggregate to take the Spanish Supercup. Leo scored three goals and assisted on the other two. Barcelona's team success continued into the UEFA Super Cup, where he scored and assisted in a 2-0 victory over Porto.

In late September, Leo became the second highest goal scorer in Barcelona's club history in a game against Racing Santander. He was second on Barcelona's La Liga goal scoring list with 132 goals. Within a few weeks, he scored his 200th goal for Barcelona in a hat-trick against Viktoria Pizen. In the Club World Cup Final, Leo was named "Man of the Match" and given the Golden Ball for his outstanding performances during the tournament. He scored two goals in the final match against Santos.

Upon year's end, Leo was awarded the UEFA Best Player in Europe Award and the Ballon d'Or for 2011, topping Xavi and Ronaldo. By earning his third Ballon d'Or, Leo became only the fourth man in history to accomplish the feat. He also became the second player to win the award three consecutive times. To complete his list of accolades, he was also given the IFFHS World's Top Goal Scorer award.

Leo continued his climb up the record books after the winter break, appearing in his 200th La Liga match in late February, in which he scored four goals. After putting up four goals in a match multiple times, Leo became the first player in Champions League history to score five goals during a single match. The match was a 7-1 trouncing of Bayer Leverkusen.

In late March, Leo scored a hat-trick against Granada, making him Barcelona's leading goal scorer in all official competitions. The accomplishment was widely celebrated among Barcelona fans, as Leo had passed club legend, Cesar Rodriguez.

Barcelona defeated Milan in the Champions League quarterfinal, before losing to Chelsea in the semifinal round. Leo posted a brace from penalty kicks against Milan, but went scoreless in the match with Chelsea, including a missed penalty kick that would have put Barcelona on top on aggregate. Nonetheless, he surpassed his personal record of twelve goals in a single Champions League season during the tournament.

A few more notable performances at the end of Leo's 2011-2012 season include a goal and two assists against Getafe CF in April and a hat-trick against Malaga CF in May, making him the highest single-season goal scorer in Europe's history. Then, after scoring four goals against RCD Espanyol, Leo's tally for the season reached seventy-two. He became the second player in history to pass the seventy goal mark in a season, only done by Archie Stark, almost a century before.

Despite all of his personal success, Leo had his eyes set on team victories - one reason his teammates love him so much. Barcelona was able to win the 2012 Copa del Rey, once more, in which Leo scored a goal in the final match. After coming up short in the final round the year before, Leo and his teammates were able to bounce back to the top.

Leo's incredible statistical accomplishments for the 2011-2012 season include setting a record of fifty goals scored in La Liga play. He was second in total assists during La Liga, with sixteen. In the Champions League, he was the top scorer and one of the leaders in assists during the tournament, with five. He finished all competitive play with a tally of seventy-three goals scored and twenty-nine goals assisted.

Leo tied for second, alongside Ronaldo, in the 2012 UEFA Best Player in Europe award. However, the moment was bittersweet for Leo, as his teammate, Andres Iniesta, was given the prestigious award, instead. Leo's season started with two consecutive braces, followed by an assist on an only goal and then two more braces against Getafe and Spartak Moscow. By mid-September, he had already totaled ten goals for the season.

After a brace against RCD Mallorca, Leo surpassed Pele's incredible milestone of seventy-five goals in a calendar year, set over five decades prior. In early November, Leo was only nine goals short of Gerd Muller's all-time single year scoring record. After a brace against Real Zaragoza, another brace against Spartak Moscow, a third against Levante UD, and a fourth against Athletic Bilbao, Leo was only one goal away from the record. In one of the most anticipated games of the year, Leo surpassed Muller's record by posting a brace against Real Betis. Leo had also surpassed Cesar Rodriguez's all-time club scoring record in La Liga play.

After the emotional performance, Leo showed class by sending Muller a signed shirt that said, "With respect and admiration." Leo continued to raise his total until year's end, finishing with ninety-one goals. In one of the easiest decisions of the year for Barcelona management, the club extended Leo's contract upon year's end. Any price would be a bargain for them!

Leo was given the Ballon d'Or award for his incredible performance in 2012, ahead of Ronaldo and Iniesta. The award marked a sustained level of excellence for the Argentine, as he became the only player in the history of the sport to win the award four times. Because of this undeniable accomplishment, the global sports media began serious comparisons between Leo and the other all-time greats, including Pele and Maradona.

While these comparisons were humbling for Leo, he did not get distracted by rankings and external opinions. Instead, he continued to stay focused on his team and worked hard. In January, he scored four goals against Osasuna, becoming the eighth player to score two hundred goals in La Liga competition.

In mid-February, he reached three hundred career goals scored for Barcelona in a match against Granada CF. In a match against Deportivo de La Coruna, Leo broke Alfredo Di Stefano's El Clasico goals record of eighteen. Before his hot streak ended against Atletico

Madrid, Leo had scored thirty-three goals in twenty-one games.

Leo's first match wearing the captain's armband, came after Andres Iniesta was substituted in a match against Rayo Vallecano. Leo became the first player in history to score in consecutive matches against every team, after scoring Barcelona's second goal at Celta de Vigo. It was also his nineteenth consecutive La Liga match with a goal scored.

In April, Leo suffered a hamstring injury, during a match against Paris Saint-Germain. His injury hampered him during the next few months, forcing him to leave during some matches. After it was announced he might miss the remainder of the season, he showed a valiant effort by entering a match in the second half of the Champions League quarterfinal second leg. He was key in setting up Pedro's game-tying goal, helping the team advance to the semifinal round.

After being eliminated by Bayern Munich in the semifinal round of the Champions League, Barcelona lost in the semifinal round of Copa del Rey. However, the team was able to capture success, taking back the La Liga title from Real

Madrid. Despite a disappointing end to his season, Leo finished as La Liga's top scorer for the second straight year, while also accumulating twelve total assists. For the entire year, he scored sixty goals and assisted sixteen times. While short of his astronomical 2011-2012 statistics, Leo's 2012-2013 season was still impressive by any player's standards.

Leo came in second place behind Ribery in the UEFA Best Player in Europe Award voting for 2013. He started the 2013-14 season with a bang, helping Barcelona win the Supercopa de Espana title over Atletico Madrid. Following a hat-trick against Valencia CF, Leo became the sixth highest goal scorer in La Liga history, surpassing Quini. After another hat-trick in Barcelona's first Champions League victory, Leo moved to second on the all-time scoring list in Champions League history. He became the first player to have at least four hat-tricks in Champions League play.

Just as he was gaining momentum, Leo suffered another injury in mid-November. The injury kept him out of competition until January. Until that point, he was still trying to regain full health, while dealing with various lingering injuries throughout the early season. However, in his first match back, Leo put up a brace in

Barcelona's 4-0 Copa del Rey victory over Getafe.

A few days later, Leo came in second place behind Ronaldo for the Ballon d'Or award, ending his streak of four consecutive victories. In mid-February, Leo overtook Alfredo di Stefano and tied Raul for the third highest goal total in La Liga history. Another record was set when Leo scored a hat-trick in March, making him Barcelona's top goal scorer in all competitions combined. By the end of the month, after a hat-trick against Real Madrid, Leo stood alone atop the all-time El Clasico goal scoring list. Simultaneously, he became the second highest goal scorer in La Liga history.

Despite a busy year climbing the record books, Barcelona faired an average season by the team's standards. They won the Spanish Super Club, but finished runner-up in La Liga. They also lost in the quarterfinal round of the Champions League. Though they made it to the final round of Copa del Rey, Barcelona lost to its rival, Real Madrid. Leo was the top scorer in the competition. At season's end, he totaled forty-one goals and fifteen assists over all competitions.

Chapter 3:

Personal Adult Life

While Leo is one of the most intriguing players on the football field, he is also an interesting character outside of it. He is a quiet and private person outside of his media obligations, though his teammates and coaches throughout the years have said very kind things regarding his personality.

While he is in a position of admiration by most soccer fans around the world, Leo is known for being personable when interacting with his supporters. He treats legends of the game, especially those who are much older than he is, with a great deal of respect.

A love for football runs in Leo's family, even in his extended family. He has two cousins professionally involved in the sport. Emanuel Biancucchi plays midfielder for Independiente F.B.C. of Paraguay, and Maxi plays winger for Club Olimpia of Paraguay.

Although Leo had been linked romantically to models from the country of his birth, namely Luciana Salazar and Macarena Ramos, he still longed for the one person he knew since he was a child and he left in Argentina, while he was growing up. That person is the lovely Antonella Rocuzzo. Leo and Antonella knew each other since they were five years old, but it was through his best friend, Lucas Scaglia, he met Antonella, Lucas' cousin.

Leo and Antonella started their romantic relationship in early 2008 and kept it private. It was only during an interview in January of 2009 that Leo confirmed his romance with his childhood sweetheart. A month after his confirmation, Leo and Antonella went public. They were seen at a carnival in Sitges, where Leo had just finished playing for Barcelona against Espanyol.

It was only after three years that they started their own family with their first child, Thiago, born in November 2012. But even before Thiago was born, Leo somehow gave the world a clue of what a wonderful blessing was about to happen to him and his girlfriend.

During a goal in a World Cup qualifying match against Ecuador, where Argentina won with a score of 4-0, Leo held the ball and tucked it under his jersey. Two weeks later, he confirmed in an interview that the gesture was a tribute to Antonella, who was pregnant with his child. On the day Thiago was born, Leo was permitted to miss his training, considering that Thiago is his first child.

On the same day, Leo proved to the world that he was the happiest man alive and shared his thoughts with the public by announcing his son on Facebook, also exclaiming his son was God's gift to the family. Leo even had his first born son's handprints and name tattooed on his left calf muscle.

Despite moving away in his early teenage years, Leo continued to hold Rosario dear to his heart. He has been keeping his Rosarino accent distinct. In addition, Leo has maintained ownership of the family's old house in Rosario, although his family no longer resides there. His Leo Messi charitable organization is also based in Rosario.

Leo has greatly tried to maintain the personal relationships from his youth, never forgetting where he came from. This includes his relationship with his "The Machine of '87" teammates. "The Machine of 87" is still relatively intact, as Leo enjoys calling and texting some of his former teammates on a fairly regular basis.

Whenever he gets to spend time in Argentina, Leo tries to meet his family and friends as much as possible, even once making a six hour round trip car drive from Buenos Aires, where he was practicing with the national team, to Rosario, in less than twenty-four hours. His mother lives in a penthouse apartment that Leo has bought for her, as his father lives mostly in Spain.

As one of the most marketable players in the sport, Leo has collaborated with many companies. In 2012, he became a global ambassador for Turkish Airlines. He has done many commercials for the company, even working with basketball legend, Kobe Bryant. In the advertisement with Kobe, Leo was trying to engage the Los Angeles Lakers star in a selfie competition. Proof of Leo's popularity was the ad's YouTube video, which received over 137 million views in the year of its release. Because of this opportunity, Leo has established a good relationship with Kobe, who told Leo he is a huge football fan and really admires his abilities.

Besides Turkish Airlines, Lionel has collaborated with the Japanese facewash, Scalp-D, and Samsung, appearing in advertisements for both. His latest and one of his biggest collaborations has been with Gillette, in which he teamed up with Swiss tennis star, Roger Federer. Soon after, Leo was announced as the face of the company's global football campaign. He is also sponsored by Adidas, EA Sports, and Pepsi, among others.

Another proof that Leo has become a part of the world's popular culture was a replica of his left foot in solid gold. Weighing 55 pounds, the replica was valued at $5.5 million and was sold in Japan in 2013. The funds were used to aid the victims of the earthquake and tsunami that hit the province of Tohoku in 2011.

Leo's global relevance can be demonstrated by his having been named to the "Time 100" list two times in his career, 2011 and 2012. The list features the one hundred most important people, as determined by *Time Magazine*, during the calendar year. On social media, Leo surpassed the fifty million follower mark in 2013. Also in 2013, he was ranked by *SportsPro* behind Neymar, the young phenomenon, as the second most marketable athlete in the world.

Chapter 4:

Philanthropic/Charitable Acts

Leo has used his fame and global platform for more than just personal glory. He has also made it a point to give back to those who are less fortunate. In 2007, he created the Leo Messi Foundation. The foundation's chief purpose is to help provide opportunities for disadvantaged children. The foundation helps in a wide range of areas, including increasing access to education and improving health care for children, who do not come from resourceful backgrounds.

As someone who dealt with a serious health issue throughout his own youth, Leo is sensitive to these children's cases. Almost parallel to his own life path, the foundation offers Argentine children in need of medical treatment and opportunities to come to Spain, where their transportation and medical costs are covered. Over the years, Leo has received partners in his mission, including Herbalife and Gillette.

Outside of his own foundation, Leo has been active in multiple other campaigns he believes in. Most notably, he was named a goodwill ambassador by UNICEF in 2010. His focus is to help the fight for children's rights in areas where they are being neglected. After Leo was appointed to this position within UNICEF, Barcelona backed his efforts.

He has also funded the construction of a new dormitory and gymnasium inside of Newell's stadium, the youth academy he attended as a youngster. In 2013, he donated 600,000 Euros to the refurbishment efforts of a children's hospital in Rosario. His financial contribution even stretched to paying for doctors to travel from Argentina to Barcelona to further their training.

After hearing about the tragedies in Syria, Leo donated 100,000 Euros to help the children of the area, staying true to his commitment to further children's rights around the world.

Leo's philosophy regarding philanthropy is something we can all learn from. His deep love for helping children is honorable, and it shows that he remembers how it felt to be a child needing medical help. Now that he has the resources and fame to make an impact, he has not only helped further some important causes, but has brought awareness to these issues because of his large outreach via social media.

Just like him, we can identify the struggles that we have faced or are currently dealing with, and use our own time, resources, and influence to help others in similar situations!

Chapter 5:

Legacy, Potential & Inspiration

While Leo hopefully still has a long career left ahead of him, he has already cemented a legacy as one of the greatest football players the world has ever seen. While legends such as Pele and Eusebio will always be favored over new generation stars, like Leo and Cristiano Ronaldo, there is no argument when it comes to the record books.

Despite his short stature, Leo has learned to compensate in other areas of the game. He has adopted a quick, relentless attacking style that creates opportunities for himself and his teammates. As mentioned earlier, his playing style has often been compared to Diego Maradona. Because he cannot use a powerful frame, instead he focuses on leveraging his low center of gravity. This allows him to be in great control of his feet and body, a key reason he never seems to be off-balance or out of position on the field.

Leo's strong legs give him the ability to quickly burst past defenders, while his impeccable footwork and ball-handling skills allow him to retain possession of the ball while dribbling. As a testament to how well he controls the ball, there is seemingly no drop-off in speed from when Leo is running, with or without the ball. He is comfortable attacking from the center of the pitch or from either wing. Perhaps, the greatest compliment of Leo's skill-set is that a manager could put him almost anywhere on the field and he would be an effective player.

While he is naturally a left-footed player, Leo has developed tremendous passing, shooting, and dribbling skills with both feet. One of the aspects of Leo's game that fans love the most is his ability to take the ball from the halfway line and dribble all the way to a beautiful goal.

However, Leo doesn't allow his supreme individual skills to deter his teammates from feeling important. He has harnessed the attention he draws from defenses into creating open shots for his teammates, as shown by his consistently high assist totals for such an aggressive player. Alongside Xavi and Iniesta, Leo has worked to form one of the most prolific offensive attacks the sport has ever seen.

Perhaps greater than his football skills however, is the great praise from the people Leo has come across during his career. Leo has a tremendous ability to make his teammates and coaches feel like they are part of his success. While he enjoys the personal success he has achieved, his main focus is always on team performance. This humility and dedication to the bigger purpose is what fans love so much about this boyish looking superstar. No matter how many trophies he has or how many records he breaks, you can count on Leo to wake up early to practice as if he has never seen glory.

His work ethic is something we can all learn from and apply to our own lives. While there are players who are more naturally talented - bigger, faster, stronger - than him, you will be hard-pressed to find a player who outworks him. He never let his lack of height, or that he was almost cut from the Barcelona youth program, stop him from becoming a professional. Instead, he

focused on what he could control and let the rest
fall where it may.

Conclusion

Hopefully this book helped you gain inspiration from the life of Lionel Messi, one of the best football players in the world.

Leo serves as a great representative for Argentina, Spain, and the sport of football. His respectful demeanor and understanding of the legends before him makes it hard for someone to dislike him. He can keep casual fans glued to the television, because they know that any time he plays, there is a possibility he will make history.

Leo has inspired so many people, because he is the star who never fails to connect with fans and give back to the less fortunate. Noted for his ability to dominate the competition on any day, he is a joy to watch on the field. Lastly, he's remarkable for remaining simple and firm with his principles, despite his immense popularity.

Hopefully you've learned some great things about Leo in this book and can apply some of the lessons you've learned to your own life! Good luck in your own journey!

38982231R00040

Made in the USA
Middletown, DE
02 January 2017